red hot salsa

red hot salsa

BILINGUAL POEMS on BEING YOUNG and LATINO in THE UNITED STATES

Edited by

Lori Marie Carlson

Introduction by

Oscar Hijuelos

Henry Holt and Company • New York

Acknowledgments

Many thanks to editors Kate Farrell and Laura Godwin
at Henry Holt and Company, and to Jennifer Lyons,
my agent, at Writers House.

Henry Holt and Company, LLC
Publishers since 1866
175 Fifth Avenue
New York, New York 10010
www.henryholtchildrensbooks.com

Library of Congress Cataloging-in-Publication Data
Red hot salsa: bilingual poems on being young and latino in the United
States / edited by Lori M. Carlson ; with an introduction by Oscar Hijuelos.—
1st ed.
p.   cm.
ISBN-13: 978-0-8050-7616-5
ISBN-10: 0-8050-7616-6
1. American poetry—Hispanic American authors.   2. Hispanic Americans—
Poetry.   I. Carlson, Lori M.
PS591.H58R43 2005   811.008'0868—dc22   2004054005

First Edition—2005 / Design by Trish Parcell Watts
Printed in the United States of America on acid-free paper. ∞

10   9   8   7   6   5   4   3   2

In memory of Alan Solis

contents

Editor's Note by Lori Marie Carlson   xi

Introduction by Oscar Hijuelos   xv

language, identity

Spanish by Gary Soto   2
El español

I Am from Quisquella la Bella by Amiris Ramírez   8
Soy de Quisquella la bella

The Hands by Gina Valdés   10
Las manos

My Shortest Food Poem by Trinidad Sánchez, Jr.   14
Mi poema a la comida más corto

I Am Who I Am, So What by Raquel Valle Sentíes   16
Soy como soy y qué

My Graduation Speech by Tato Laviera   22

Invisible Boundaries by Ivette Álvarez   24
Límites invisibles

neighborhoods

New in New York by Carlos Aguasaco   28
Nueva en Nueva York

Beloved Spic by Martín Espada   30
Amado Spic

Armitage Street by David Hernandez   32
Calle Armitage

Life in el Barrio by Kizzilie Bonilla   36
La vida en el barrio

Leaving Ybor City by Jaime Manrique   40
Dejando Ybor City

Tumbling Through My Tumbaburro
by Jacinto Jesús Cardona   46

Calling All Chamacos! by Jacinto Jesús Cardona   47

amor

love by Gwylym Cano   50
amor

Fill My World with Music by Sandra María Esteves   52
Llena mi mundo con música

Your Eyes by Luis Alberto Ambroggio   54
Tus ojos

First Kiss by Raquel Valle Sentíes   58
El primer beso

El Parpadeo by Trinidad Sánchez, Jr.   60
El parpadeo

In Virginia Woods Near Leesburg
by Claudia Quiróz Cahill   62
En los bosques de Virginia cerca de Leesburg

Prom Poem for Jorge Barroso
by Sandra M. Castillo   66
Poema de baile de graduación para Jorge Barroso

Upon Knowing You by Yeni Herrera   70
Al conocerte

Bilingual Love Poem by José Antonio Burciaga   72
Poema de amor bilingüe

family moments, memories

Tía Chucha by Luis J. Rodríguez   76
Tía Chucha

Martin and My Father *by David Hernandez*   82
Martin y mi padre

Dead Pig's Revenge by Michele Serros   86
La venganza del chancho muerto

At a Peach Orchard in Virginia
by Claudia Quiróz Cahill   96
En una granja de duraznos en Virginia

The Piñata Painted with a Face Like Mine
by Martín Espada   100
La piñata pintada con una cara como la mía

Saturdays Set Within Memory
by Isaac Goldemberg   104
Sábado aferrado a la memoria

This Is for Mamacita by Willie Perdomo   106
Esto es para mamacita

victory

Triumph by Marjorie Agosín   112
El triunfo

In a Minute by Robert B. Feliciano   114
En un minuto

Piece by Piece by Luis J. Rodríguez   116
Pedazo a pedazo

Ode to the Tortilla by Gina Valdés   118
Oda a la tortilla

The Journey That We Are
by Luis Alberto Ambroggio   122
El viaje que somos

Look to the Sun by Sandra María Esteves   124
Mira al sol

For Bert Corona by Trinidad Sánchez, Jr.   126

Glossary   127

Biographical Notes   133

editor's note

BY LORI MARIE CARLSON

It is always somewhat risky to follow up an anthology like *Cool Salsa* with a second volume. For years I hesitated to do so, as I felt I had, in that book, met my goal of providing American youth with a poetic look at what it's like to grow up in the United States, as seen through the eyes of our country's vibrant Latino community in all its complexity, ethnic variation, linguistic diversity and yearning spirit.

Then, one day while riding the 104 bus down Broadway in New York City, I overheard a lively conversation among a group of Latina teens that intrigued me. They were talking about Ricky Martin. Well, not really talking. Rhapsodizing would be more like it. A group of girls talking in a mix of languages, in a streety English hip-hop and a swoony lyricism spiked with Spanish.

Ten years before, Ricky Martin, while popular, was not yet the sensation he would become. There was no Latino superstar singer on the scene for girls their age to dream and gush about back then. Now he was a superstar in two worlds, one dominated by English and the other by Spanish.

In that moment, I realized that I had been wrong about not pursuing a sequel volume to *Cool Salsa*. Since 1994, so very much has changed in the United States vis-à-vis the Latino population.

One of the obvious outcomes of the Latin American immigration to this land is the acknowledgment by our society and the media of the amazing contributions of Latinos of all walks of life and ethnicities to the dynamism of the nation. In the fields of science, arts and letters, military service, public affairs, entertainment, fashion, and food, Latin Americans and Latinos of several generations are offering our country their best. And they are helping to transform the notion of what it means to be a proud American.

The contributions of Latino writers to the American canon continue to grow. This is particularly true of Latino poets. There is so much exceptional poetry being published today—so much that in my meanderings through libraries, schools, cultural institutions, bookstores, and churches, I found myself dizzied by the offerings.

And yet for all the gains Latinos have begun to experience, there remains an entrenched sense that they are also apart from the mainstream. Time and again, in my conversations and daily activities, I find that Latinos continue to suffer feelings of alienation from the power structures that fuel so many aspects of our society.

Historically speaking, all immigrant groups have known feelings of separateness, prejudice, and injustice. But the Latino experience is unique, as so much of our country was at one time under Spanish or Mexican rule and influenced powerfully by the Spanish language. Thus, for not a few who claim Mexican and Iberian antecedents, there is a sense of having lost something that once existed in a vivid, life-affirming way.

And, then, there is the issue of the border, a particularly wrenching reminder for those who live in states where the U.S. and Mexico share earth. The spine of that common earth is hurting.

What, today, are Latino poets saying to us? *Red Hot Salsa* offers diverse bilingual answers. In this collection, poets from across America, in small towns such as Leesburg, Virginia; Golden, Colorado; and Wellesley, Massachusetts—and cities such as Miami, Boston, Chicago, Los Angeles, San Antonio, and New York are telling us who they are, how and where they live, the significance of family, and what their dreams are for the future.

There are quite a few poets in this collection who appeared in *Cool Salsa,* among them Gary Soto, Martín Espada, Trinidad Sánchez, Jr., Gina Valdés, and Luis J. Rodríguez. But there are also new voices and younger voices, among them an eloquent teen whom I met at a gathering at the New York Society Library.

The translations have been penned for the most part by the poets in this collection, along with several of my translations. Just as in *Cool Salsa,* some poems have not been translated but appear only once in their hybrid linguistic beauty.

And, again, the Pulitzer prize–winning novelist Oscar Hijuelos has written an introduction befitting the music and heart of these poets' words.

I hope *Red Hot Salsa* takes you farther on a journey that began ten years ago with *Cool Salsa* in the spirit of friendship, solidarity, and gratitude.

introduction
BY OSCAR HIJUELOS

Although I have come to love the process of writing, it was not what I would have predicted for myself, nor did it come easily. For one thing, growing up in a working-class household on the Upper West Side of New York City, I was not surrounded by books. I had no sense of what literature was about.

My parents came to the U.S. in the mid-1940s from Cuba with the equivalent of high school diplomas, but when they arrived in this country they had little, if any, knowledge of English. Although they both learned to speak English, they spoke mainly Spanish in our home.

My own relationship to Spanish is, no doubt, connected to the fact that I became a writer: my first language was Spanish, but when I was four I contracted a kidney disease and spent a year and a half in various hospitals and convalescent homes recuperating. According to my mother, I "went into the hospital speaking Spanish, and came out speaking English." The upshot was that my parents spoke to me in Spanish, and I responded in English.

I grew up in a state of linguistic confusion. Neither "here nor there," I always felt ill-prepared, underqualified, about both English and Spanish.

In grammar school I read whatever was assigned to me and always had respect for my teachers, Sinsinawa Dominican nuns, but never did I feel particularly confident about myself, no matter what my grades were like. I was always surprised to pass into the next grade, and while I did well enough, I could never escape the sense that I would never catch up to the rest of the students. When it came to English, there were always words I had never heard before. Once, while in the fourth grade at Corpus Christi school, I received a Valentine's card that said "I think you're cute." Because I had no idea of what "cute" meant, I asked my mother, who seemed to think it had some relation to the Spanish word "cutis" for complexion.

Of course, we did have our share of English to read: the New York *Daily News* (along with the Spanish language *El Diario*), but what literature entered our Upper West Side apartment seemed arbitrary, books that had been left under the stairwell by college students (we lived in a Columbia University neighborhood). *Trends in American Agricultural Technology, 1956–1957*, is a title I can remember, as well as many a textbook and the occasional tattered, disintegrating novel that seemed valuable because of its ornate, gold-leafed spine—Galsworthy comes to mind—books whose prose and rich vocabulary seemed so dense and indecipherable and intimidating that we only used them as decorative objects to adorn a hallway bookshelf. We also had an encyclopedia, my salvation, a World Book set that my mother had ordered because the priestly, very handsome salesman was a Cuban fellow trying to work his way through college. (She says that's not true!)

Along the way, as I entered my teens I was introduced to the occasional sci-fi and Tarzan novel by Edgar Rice Burroughs, the urban novels of Harlem writers like Chester Himes and Iceberg Slim. There were also some quasi-pornographic Victorian works (well, let's say bluntly porno-graphic, like *My Life and Loves* by Frank Harris) that were passed about for their randy content among the scruffy kids of the neighborhood. But I did not read Jane Austen or Charles Dickens or Thomas Hardy or, for that matter, any of the great Spanish novelists or poets—no Miguel de Cervantes, no Francisco de Quevedo—nothing.

Most of my friends were of mixed ethnicities—Puerto Rican and Cuban, Irish and Italian and African Haitian and African American—and spoke mainly English, an English that was greatly informed by the streety, black-intoned dialect of New York City. (Think "Jive.") Given that we lived on the cusp of a university neighborhood— we were "townies," as it were. With our proximity to Barnard and Columbia and with a number of cluttered bookstores dotting Broadway and Amsterdam Avenues, I should have felt a natural inclination toward books and reading. Certainly, there were enough bookish-looking students and their professors around to provide an inspi-ration. But the truth is that education begins at home, and while my mother and father were both bright people and raised me to respect my teachers, I can never recall having a single day of feeling any kind of real confi-dence in regards to my own abilities.

One day, at the age of seventeen, I turned around to find that my father had dropped dead from overwork (two jobs for twenty-five years). Filled with a rage about life, I left home and never really returned. After that I spent years stumbling around, dropping in and out of school.

I went to college, but I found little to interest me, and I could never really concentrate on my studies. But one afternoon, in the course of writing a theme for a basic composition class at Bronx Community, I made a few sentences that, in their own way, seemed accomplished and interesting. It wasn't much, but it suggested a possible direction for me—perhaps one day I would teach English in high school, I had thought—but that was all. The more I wrote, however, the more I began to take pride in what I was doing, a new feeling for me. And my confidence increased a bit.

Still, I did not think that I would become a writer. I saw my classes in English literature and the occasional writing workshop as a way of getting through school. I do know that I liked the idea of excelling in English, perhaps as a compensation for my relative loss of Spanish.

Luck and the way things play out are unpredictable. After starting my college years at Bronx Community, then going to Lehman College night school, then to Manhattan Community College for a semester, I matriculated into CCNY, the Harvard of the working class, as a junior. And that school was a revelation of voices and energies. As a multi-ethnic commuter college, its classrooms were filled with immigrants or the children of immigrants like me. Its writing workshops were especially interesting because so many diverse points of view and personal histories, along with quirky linguistics, came forward during those sessions. Best of all were the teachers at City. Open-minded and intent upon mining the richness of their students' experiences, they created an atmosphere in which even someone who had always been timid about his scholastic and creative abilities began to develop a true interest in becoming a writer.

I imagine that the writers in *Red Hot Salsa* might have had experiences similar to my own. In any event, the worlds they describe are, from my point of view, very familiar. Their intense feelings about survival and "becoming" are palpable on the page. And the Spanish/English versions of their poetry equally beautiful, stirring, and worthy of our humanity.

language, identity

Spanish
by Gary Soto

Spanish is a matter
of rolling *rrrrr*s
Clicking the tongue,
And placing
Your hands
On your hips
When your little brother
Pours cereal
Into your fishbowl.
Spanish is a matter
Of yelling, *"¡Abuela,*
Teléfono! Una vendedora
De TV Guide."
It's a matter
Of Saturdays, too.
You enter the confessional
And whisper
To the priest
First the sins
You did in English,
Like screaming at the boy
On the blue bike,
And then muttering
Your sins in Spanish,
Like when you
Put on lipstick
And had bad thoughts about Mercedes López,
That big show-off in new jeans.
Spanish is a matter
Of *"¡Ay, Dios!"*
When the beans burn

Or *"¡Chihuahua!"*
When the weakest kid
Hits a home run.
Spanish is a matter
Of your *abuelo*
And his *compa*
Chuckling about their younger days
While playing checkers
Under the grape arbor,
Their faces lined
And dark as the earth
At their feet.
Spanish words march across
A bag of
Chicharrones,
Those salty clubs
That could easily hammer a nail
Through the wall,
They're so hard.
You've always known
Spanish, even
Behind the bars
Of your crib
When you babbled,
Mami, papi, flor, cocos—
Nonsense in the middle of the night.
At school, your friends
Have to learn Spanish,
Tripping over *gato,*
Y perro, easy words
You learned
When you looked out
The back window.
You're good at Spanish,
And even better at math.

When you walk home,
Dragging a stick
Through the rain puddles,
Spanish is seeing double.
The world is twice the size
And, with each year,
With one more candle
On a crooked cake,
Getting bigger.

El español
por Gary Soto
translated from the English by Carlos Aguasaco

El español es cuestión
de echar a rodar las *rrrrrs*
Pulsar la lengua
y poner
tus manos
en las caderas
cuando tu hermanito
vierte cereal
en tu pecera.
El español es cuestión
de gritar, "¡Abuela,
Teléfono! Una vendedora
de *TV Guide*."
También es cuestión
de sábado.
Entras al confesionario
y le susurras
al sacerdote
primero los pecados
que cometiste en inglés,
como gritarle al chico
de la bicicleta azul,
y luego mascullar
tus pecados en español,
como cuando
te pusiste pintalabios
y tuviste malos pensamientos de Mercedes López,
ese gran alarde en jeans nuevos.
El español es cuestión
de exclamar "¡Ay, Dios!"
cuando se queman las habichuelas

o "¡Chihuahua!"
cuando el chico más débil
batea un cuadrangular.
El español es cuestión
de tu *abuelo*
y su *compa*
riéndose entre dientes de su juventud
mientras juegan damas
bajo la parra,
sus caras arrugadas
y oscuras como la tierra
a sus pies.
Las palabras españolas marchan
en una bolsa de
chicharrones,
esos palitos salados
que podrían facilmente clavar una puntilla
a través del muro
son tan duros.
Siempre has sabido
español, incluso
detrás de las rejas
de tu cuna
cuando balbuceabas
Mami, papi, flor, cocos—
incoherencias en el medio de la noche.
En la escuela, tus amigos
tienen que aprender español,
tropezándose con *gato*
y *perro*, palabras fáciles
que aprendiste
cuando mirabas
por la ventana de atrás.
Eres bueno en español,
y aún mejor en matemáticas.

Cuando caminas a casa,
arrastrando un palo
por los charcos,
El español es ver doble.
El mundo es dos veces más grande
y, con cada año,
con una vela más
en un pastel torcido
sigue creciendo.

I Am from Quisquella la Bella
by Amiris Ramírez

I am
from *Quisquella la bella,*
from *merengue, bachata, perico ripiao,*
and church bells on Sundays.

I am
from the words
Dios, patria, libertad
from the feeling of sadness, but also of not giving up.

I am
from the promise of friendship and love,
from "always be yourself,"
"believe in who you are."

I am
from rice and beans,
roast chicken, *pernil,*
plátanos, mangos, coconuts, corn.

I am
from beautiful
gardens with palm trees,
from mountains and precious blue sky.

I am Latina.
Dominican.
Proud.

Soy de Quisquella la bella

por Amiris Ramírez

translated from the English by L. M. Carlson

Soy
de Quisquella la bella,
de merengue, bachata, perico ripiao,
y campanillas
los domingos.

Soy
de las palabras
Dios, patria, libertad,
de tristeza, pero también de potencia.

Soy
de la promesa de amistad y amor,
de "siempre sé tú,"
"cree en ti misma."

Soy
de arroz y frijoles,
pollo asado, pernil,
plátanos, mangos, cocos, maíz.

Soy de bellos
jardines con palmas reales,
de montañas y precioso cielo azul.

Soy latina.
Dominicana.
Orgullosa.

The Hands
by Gina Valdés

translated from the Spanish by Gina Valdés

Depending on the light, of the hairy
sun or of the moon, of the shade
of a tamarind at noon or a chapel
at dusk, the hands, these hands,
my hands, your hands, will appear
cream or cinnamon, pink, red, black
or yellow—our heritage.

These are hands of congas,
of requintos, güiros, claves, bongos
and timbales, of maracas, charangos,
guitarrones and marimbas,
castanets, tambourines and cymbals,
tin tin timbaleo tingo
these hands sing, dance, clap
to the beat of corn rumbeando
on its way to becoming a tortilla,
these hands round albóndigas and dreams,
circle waists, sighs and hips,
peel bananas, masks and mangos,
add, subtract, multiply on blackboards,
beds and griddles, these hands speak
fluent Spanish, they warm,
they reduce fevers, sometimes they write
poetry, sometimes they recite it,
these hands could take
away all pain.

These hands, tied by centuries of rope
to ovens, to tables and to diapers, to
brooms, mops, trays and dusters,

to saws and hammers, to picks, shovels,
and hoes, they scrub floors,
plates and lies, pick strawberries,
grapes, insults and onions,
plant corn, mint, cilantro and hope,
piece by piece they unearth
our history.

These hands, so large, so small,
two hummingbirds, quiet, still, joined,
pierced by a nail of U.S. steel, unbind, shout,
close into a fist of sorrow, of anger,
of impatience, these raised hands
open, demand the same as they produce,
as they are giving, these hands smile
in triumph.

Las manos
por Gina Valdés

Según la luz, del sol greñudo
o de la luna, de la sombra
de un tamarindo al mediodía
o de una capilla al atardecer,
las manos, estas manos, mis manos,
tus manos, se verán color de crema
o de canela, rosa, rojas, negras
o amarillas—nuestra herencia.

Estas son manos de congas,
de requintos, güiros, claves, bongós
y timbales, de maracas, charangos,
guitarrones y marimbas,
castañuelas, panderetas y címbalos,
tin tin timbaleo tingo
estas manos cantan, bailan, palmean
al son del maíz rumbeando
rumbo a ser tortilla,
estas manos redondean albóndigas
y sueños, circundan cinturas,
suspiros y caderas, pelan plátanos,
máscaras y mangos, suman, restan,
multiplican en pizarras, en camas
y en comales, estas manos
hablan español con soltura,
calientan y quitan calentura,
a veces escriben poesía,
a veces la recitan, estas manos
pudieran quitar todas
las penas.

Estas manos, atadas con siglos de cuerdas
a hornos, a mesas y pañales,
a escobas, trapeadores, bandejas y plumeros,
a serruchos y martillos, a picos,
palas y azadones, restriegan pisos,
platos y mentiras, recogen fresas,
uvas, insultos y cebollas, siembran
maíz, yerbabuena, cilantro y esperanza,
poco a poco desentierran
nuestra historia.

Estas manos, tan inmensas, tan pequeñas,
dos chuparrosas, atadas, quietas,
atravesadas por un clavo de acero americano,
se desatan, gritan, se cierran en un puño
de amargura, de coraje, de impaciencia,
estas manos alzadas se abren,
exigen lo mismo que producen,
que están dando, estas manos
sonríen en su triunfo.

My Shortest Food Poem
by Trinidad Sánchez, Jr.

Taco Bell
is NOT
Mexican food!

Mi poema a la comida más corto
por Trinidad Sánchez, Sr.

translated from the English by L. M. Carlson

¡Taco Bell
NO es
comida mexicana!

I Am Who I Am, So What
by Raquel Valle Senties

translated from the Spanish by Raquel Valle Senties

I'm a grafted flower that didn't
take, a Mexican without being one,
an American without feeling like one.

The music of my people fills me.
The huapangos, rancheras,
and the Mexican National Anthem
give me goose bumps, a lump
in my throat. They make my feet tap
to the beat. But I feel as if I'm wearing
a borrowed hat.
Mexicans stare as if saying,
   "You're not a Mexican!"

The "Star-Spangled Banner" also
gives me goose bumps,
a lump in my throat.
Gringos stare as if saying,
"You're not an American!"
My soul crumples.
My heart has no room for two
countries as it has no room
for two lovers.
Not from here, not from there,
not Mexican enough,
not American enough.

I'll have to say,
I'm from the border,
   from Laredo,
from a strange place

neither Mexican nor American,
where at sunset the smell of
fajitas grilled over mesquite
makes my mouth water,
where on birthdays
we sing "Happy Birthday"
and *"Las mañanitas."*
Where we celebrate George
Washington's birthday—who
knows why?
Where outsiders get culture
shock and can live here fifty
years and still be outsiders;
where in many places the
green, white and red flag
waves proudly beside
the red, white and blue.

Displaced like the Río
Grande, once a part of Mexico,
a puppet jerked by the strings
of two cultures that clash. I'm
la mestiza
la pocha,
la Tex-Mex,
la Mexican-American,
la hyphenated
who lacks identity
and struggles to find it,
who no longer wants to
ignore a reality
that strikes her,
that wounds her,
who no longer wants
to bite her tongue,

who in Veracruz defended
the United States with
volcanic passion,
who in Laredo defends
México the same way.

I am a walking contradiction.
In other words, like Laredo,
I am who I am. So what?

Soy como soy y qué
por Raquel Valle Sentíes

Soy flor injertada que no pegó.
Soy mexicana sin serlo.
Soy americana sin sentirlo.
La música de mi pueblo,
la que me llena,
los huapangos, las rancheras,
el himno nacional mexicano,
hace que se me enchine el cuero,
que se me haga un nudo en la garganta,
que bailen mis pies al compás,
pero siento como quien se pone
sombrero ajeno.
Los mexicanos me miran como diciendo
¡Tú no eres mexicana!

El himno nacional de EE.UU.
también hace
que se me enchine el cuero,
que se me haga un nudo
en la garganta.
Los gringos me miran
como diciendo,
¡Tú no eres americana!
Se me arruga el alma.
En mí no caben dos patrias
como no cabrían dos amores.
Desgraciadamente,
no me siento ni de aquí,
ni de allá.

Ni suficientemente mexicana.
Ni suficientemente americana.
Tendré que decir:
Soy de la frontera.
De Laredo.
De un mundo extraño,
ni mexicano,
ni americano.
Donde al caer la tarde
el olor a fajitas asadas con mesquite,
hace que se le haga a uno agua la boca.

Donde en el cumpleaños
lo mismo cantamos
el Happy Birthday que las mañanitas.
Donde festejamos en grande
el nacimiento de Jorge Washington
¿quién sabe por qué?
Donde a los foráneos
les entra culture shock
cuando pisan Laredo
y podrán vivir cincuenta años
aquí y seguirán siendo
foráneos.
Donde en muchos lugares
la bandera verde, blanca y colorada
vuela orgullosamente
al lado de la red, white and blue.

Soy como el Río Grande,
una vez parte de México,
desplazada.
Soy como un títere
jalado por los hilos de dos culturas

que chocan entre sí.
Soy la mestiza,
la pocha,
la Tex-Mex, la Mexican-American
la hyphenated,
la que sufre
por no tener identidad propia
y lucha por encontrarla,
la que ya no quiere cerrar los ojos
a una realidad que golpea,
que hiere,
la que no quiere andarse con tiento,
la que en Veracruz
defendía a EE.UU.
con uñas y dientes.
La que en Laredo
defiende a México
con uñas y dientes.
Soy la contradicción andando.

En fin, como Laredo,
soy como soy y qué.

My Graduation Speech
by Tato Laviera

i think in spanish
i write in english

i want to go back to puerto rico,
but i wonder if my kink could live
in ponce, mayagüez and carolina

tengo las venas aculturadas
escribo en spanglish
abraham in español

abraham in english
tato in spanish
"taro" in english
tonto in both languages

how are you?
¿cómo estás?
i don't know if I'm coming
or si me fui ya

si me dicen barranquitas, yo reply,
"¿con qué se come eso?"
si me dicen caviar, i digo,
"a new pair of converse sneakers."

ahí supe que estoy jodío
ahí supe que estamos jodíos

english or spanish
spanish or english
spanenglish
now, dig this:

hablo lo inglés matao
hablo lo español matao
no sé leer ninguno bien

so it is, spanglish to matao
what i digo
¡ay, virgen, yo no sé hablar!

Invisible Boundaries
by Ivette Álvarez

I'm surrounded by a society that expects nothing of me
   other than to become a regular, tired housewife.
   I speak my mind and it's considered rude.
When I speak with my peers
   I'm told that I speak like
   a white girl.
Don't they realize we could
   go beyond the stereotypes that
   lock us down and judge us?
I walk the streets and I become frantic.
   I desperately want
   out of this cycle.
I refuse to have my name
   added to the list of nobodies who
   didn't become anything because they
   weren't strong enough to fight.
I want to become
   someone important. I must
   overcome the invisible boundaries.

Límites invisibles

por Ivette Álvarez

translated from the English by Luis Alberto Ambroggio

Me circunda una sociedad que no espera nada de mí
   sino el convertirme en una ama de casa normal y
cansada.
   Digo lo que pienso y me consideran maleducada.
Cuando dialogo con mis compinches
   comentan que hablo como
   una chica blanca.
¿No se dan cuenta que podríamos acaso
   traspasar los estereotipos
   que nos juzgan y nos atan?
Camino las calles y me desespero.
   Frenéticamente anhelo
   escapar de este ciclo.
Rehuso que mi nombre
   se añada a la lista de los nadies
   que devinieron en nada
   por no tener suficiente valentía para luchar.
Me propongo llegar a ser
   alguien importante. Debo
   superar los límites invisibles.

neighborhoods

New in New York

by Carlos Aguasaco

translated from the Spanish by L. M. Carlson

I like that my grandma is new in New York
I take the subway map and unfold it on the ground
I explain to my grandma that the train is a worm on
    wheels
That Manhattan is a big apple
That we enter and exit by way of subterranean holes

My grandma touches my forehead and asks if I have a
    fever
I answer that my tattoo is necessary to be *cool*
My brother tells her that *cool* means cold like *ice cream*
I tell her that *cool* means *happy* like in *happy birthday*
My grandmother smiles and talks about her birthday

How do I explain to my parents that my grandma wants
    a tattoo?
A tattoo with an apple and a worm like an arrow
That says "Robert's grandma loves New York,
she's cool and she's here to stay"

Nueva en Nueva York
por Carlos Aguasaco

Me gusta que mi abuela sea nueva en Nueva York
Tomo el map del subway y lo extiendo en el suelo
Le explico a mi abuela que el tren es un gusano con
    ruedas
Que Manhattan es una gran manzana
Que entramos y salimos de ella por agujeros
    subterráneos

Mi abuela lleva la mano a la frente y pregunta si tengo
    fiebre
Le digo que este tatuaje es necesario para ser *cool*
Mi hermano le dice que *cool* significa frío como el *ice
    cream*
Yo le digo que *cool* significa *happy* como en *happy
    birthday*
Mi abuela sonríe y nos habla de sus cumpleaños

¿Cómo les explico a mis padres que mi abuela quiere
    un tatuaje?
Un tatuaje de una manzana y un gusano como una
    flecha
Que dice "la abuela de Roberto ama a Nueva York,
es cool y está aquí para quedarse"

Beloved Spic

—Valley Stream, Long Island, 1973

by Martin Espada

Here in the new white neighborhood,
the neighbors kept it pressed
inside dictionaries and Bibles
like a leaf, chewed it for digestion
after a heavy dinner,
laughed when it hopped
from their mouths like a secret,
whispered it as carefully as the answer
to a test question in school,
bellowed it in barrooms
when the alcohol
made them want to sing.

So I saw it
spraypainted on my locker and told no one,
found it scripted in the icing on a cake,
touched it stinging like the tooth slammed
into a faucet, so I kept my mouth closed,
pushed it away crusted on the coach's lip
with a spot of dried egg,
watched it spiral into the ear of a disappointed girl who
      never sat
beside me again,
heard it in my head when I punched a lamp,
mesmerized by the slash oozing
between my knuckles,
and it was beloved
until the day we staked our lawn
with a sign that read: For Sale.

Amado Spic

—Valley Stream, Long Island, 1973

por Martín Espada

translated from the English by Carlos Aguasaco

Aquí en el nuevo barrio blanco,
los vecinos lo mantenían presionado
entre diccionarios y Biblias
como una hoja, lo masticaban para hacer la digestión
después de una cena pesada,
reían cuando brincaba
de sus bocas como un secreto,
lo susurraban con el mismo cuidado que
una respuesta a un examen en la escuela,
lo bramaban en los bares
cuando el alcohol
los hacía querer cantar.

De igual manera lo vi
escrito con aerosol en mi casillero y no se lo dije a nadie,
grabado en la cubierta de un pastel,
si lo tocabas dolía como un diente golpeado
contra un grifo, así que mantuve mi boca cerrada,
lo aparté de un empujón encostrado en el labio del
    entrenador
con una mancha de huevo seco,
lo observé hacer una espiral dentro de la oreja de una
    chica decepcionada
que nunca más se volvió a sentar junto a mí,
lo escuché en mi cabeza cuando golpeé una lámpara,
hipnotizado por la herida rezumante
entre mis nudillos,
y era amado
hasta el día en que estacamos nuestro césped
con un letrero que dice: Se vende.

Armitage Street
by David Hernandez

Waiting for the elevated train
during a pale, faintly cold afternoon,
I looked down on Armitage street
full of quaint old buildings,
upscale stores and fashionably dressed
mothers pushing white-walled baby carriages
on well-heeled sidewalks.

It seems just like yesterday on Armitage street
that Alfredo and Cha-Cha played hide and seek
with Quinto the cop while Cosmo and Aidita
made love in the gangway.
  When radios blared out open windows
  dressed in five and dime laced curtains.
  When staccato spanish bounced between
  buildings high above the rolling traffic
  Because telephones were insultingly impersonal
  and it was no secret that the eyes expressed the heart.
    When rice and bean
    smells
    roamed the hallways covering up
    the tracks of other ethnics who had
    since faded into the American dream.
When candles danced amber-hue
in roach sprayed apartments
from all-night vigils for the dead
before being shipped back to their homeland
in self-addressed, stamped coffins.
  And the children kissed their cheeks
  in gratitude for all the nickels and candy

after payday, for all the stories and
pony rides on laps and knees they received
and the dead knew they would be missed.
   When 25-cent haircuts at Don Florencio's
   illegal basement barber shop made you
   smell pretty, doused in brilliantine hair tonic
   ready for Sunday church services.
      And Nereida, the beautiful older cousin
      that you secretly loved, was the official translator
      for schoolteacher notes pinned to lapels and coats
      because the mothers were all englishless.
      When the last summer days were spent
      under street rainbow firehydrant showers
      and that night you overheard your parents whisper
      about moving out because the rent was going up.
But you didn't care because last autumn during school
Ms Greenspan said that someday you would be a great
      writer,
Renee finally kissed you during recess
and that was enough for any boy's lifetime.
            And to think
            It seems just like yesterday
            on Armitage street.

Calle Armitage
por David Hernandez
translated from the English by Carlos Aguasaco

Esperaba el tren elevado
en una tarde clara y ligeramente fría,
bajé la mirada hacia la calle Armitage
llena de edificios viejos y pintorescos,
tiendas costosas y madres vestidas a la moda
empujando blancos coches de bebé
por andenes para ricos.

Parece que fue ayer, en la calle Armitage,
que Alfredo y Cha-Cha jugaban al escondite
con Quinto, el policía, mientras Cosmo y Aidita
hacían el amor en el pasadizo.
    Cuando los radios retumbaban por las ventanas
      abiertas
    con cortinas de encaje de baratillo.
    Cuando el español rebotaba a pedazos entre
    los edificios por encima del tráfico
    Porque los teléfonos eran insultantemente
      impersonales
    y para nadie era un secreto que los ojos son el
      espejo del corazón.
    Cuando el olor del arroz
    con habichuelas
    vagaba por los corredores cubriendo
    los rastros de otras etnias
    que ya se habían diluido en el sueño americano.
Cuando las velas danzaban en tonos de ámbar
en apartamentos rociados de veneno para cucarachas
en los velorios de los muertos
antes de enviarlos a su tierra natal
en un ataúd con estampillas y la dirección del difunto.

Los niños besaban sus mejillas
en gratitud por los dulces y las monedas
del día de pago, por todas las historias y
todas las veces que los balancearon en sus regazos
los muertos sabían que serían extrañados.
Cuando los cortes de cabello de 25 centavos
en la barbería ilegal que Don Florencio tenía en
un sótano
te hacía oler bien, con el cabello bañado en
brillantina
listo para los servicios religiosos del domingo.
Y Nereida, la bellísima prima mayor
que amabas en secreto, era la traductora oficial
de las notas que los profesores pegaban en las
solapas
y los abrigos
porque todas las madres no hablaban inglés.
Cuando los últimos días del verano se pasaban
bajo el arco iris callejero de los hidrantes abiertos
y esa noche en que escuchaste a tus padres susurrar
que debían mudarse porque la renta estaba
subiendo.
No te importó porque el otoño anterior en la escuela
la señorita Greenspan dijo que algún día serías un
gran escritor,
Renee finalmente te besó durante el recreo
y eso era más que suficiente para la vida entera de
cualquier chico.
Y pensar
Parece que fue ayer
en la calle Armitage.

Life in el Barrio
by Kizzilie Bonilla

Yelling
banging
people throwing plates
sirens screeching
hoodlums getting thrown against gates
Hitting
slapping
crying
being loud
Drug dealers standing
outside selling proud
Alarms
Burglars lurking
in the night screaming
shouting
gangs having fights
Shoot outs
bullets flying across the sky
Nine-year-old boys on the stairwell getting high
Horns beeping
cars driving by to see
the girls on the corner
saying hi
Banging
slapping
a man shouting at his wife
Kids being so scared
killing the father with a knife
Babies crying out
please feed me

Mothers yelling
shut up kid and let me be
Sisters selling all they've got
walking with friends
smoking pot
Life in el Barrio
is like this
day in and day out
It's only the ones suffering who don't shout

La vida en el barrio

por Kizzilie Bonilla

translated from the English by Luis Alberto Ambroggio

Gritando
golpeando
la gente tirando platos
sirenas chillando
matones empujados contra las puertas
Pegando
abofeteando
llorando
siendo ruidosos
vendedores de drogas parados
afuera vendiendo orgullosos
Alarmas
Ladrones al acecho
en la noche aullando
vociferando
las patotas peleando
Absoluto tiroteo
balas volando a través del cielo
Niños de nueve años alucinándose en las escaleras
Bocinas sonando
autos paseándose para ver
las chicas en la esquina
diciendo hola
machacando
abofeteando
un hombre gritándole a su esposa
Hijos tan asustados
que matan al padre con un cuchillo
Bebés llorando
Por favor aliméntenme

Madres gritando
cállate chico y déjame vivir
Hermanas vendiéndose completas
caminando con amigas
fumando marihuana
La vida en el Barrio
es así
uno y otro día
Sólo los que están sufriendo no gritan

Leaving Ybor City
by Jaime Manrique

The summer I finished high school
Mother and I worked in the same factory
in Ybor City, the black section of town.

Mami sewed all day
in silence, she knew
only a few words in English.
I worked alone, sorting out huge containers
of soiled hospital linen
and I despised every minute of it.
I was eighteen; Mami nearly fifty.

After work, we took the bus home.
As the suffocating heat
lifted, and the mango tree
in our yard released fruity
scents and yielded shadow
the languorous stretch
before dark
was a time to forget the factory
to become human.

The apartment we lived in on Elmore Street
had linoleum floors
and termites in the furniture.
After our TV dinner
—we were so new in America these
dinners seemed another miracle of technology—
mother visited her friend Hortencia,
a Cuban refugee so overweight
she could not walk to our house

after a day of piecework.
We had no television, no telephone,
so I sat on the terrace
watched the elevated highway
next to the house and read
novels that transported me
far away from Ybor City.

On Saturday afternoons, I walked
to the old library in downtown Tampa
where I discovered, in Spanish,
Manuel Puig's *Betrayed by Rita Hayworth*.
I read this book at night
and during breaks at the factory:
a novel with a homosexual boy hero
that made me dream of glamorous
MGM Technicolor musicals and goddesses
in slinky glittering gowns.
I was young.

Sitting on the porch
as dusk deepened
punctured by fireflies
darting stars weaving
in and out of mangoes
I dreamt of distant cities
of going to college, of writing
books, of leading a life
that had nothing to do with a factory,
not knowing
I would journey
away from Ybor City
exiled from the world of my mother
yet still be a survivor.

It's only now, when I think back
on the youth I was
that I can feel
heartache for my innocence
for my mother's silent fortitude
for our unspoken fears;
for lives that were hard
but rich in dreams.

Dejando Ybor City

por Jaime Manrique

translated from the English by Carlos Aguasaco

El verano en que terminé la secundaria
Mamá y yo trabajamos en la misma fábrica
en Ybor City, la parte negra del pueblo.

Mami cosía todo el día
en silencio, sabía solamente
algunas palabras en inglés.
Yo trabajaba solo, organizando grandes contenedores
de sábanas de hospital sucias
y detestaba cada minuto de ese trabajo.
Yo tenía dieciocho y Mami casi cincuenta.

Depués del trabajo, tomábamos el autobús a casa.
Cuando el calor sofocante
Se levantaba, y el mango
de nuestro patio desprendía el aroma de su fruta
y daba sombra
el tiempo lánguido
antes de la oscuridad
era el momento para olvidar la fábrica
y volverse humano.

El apartamento en que vivíamos en la calle Elmore
tenía pisos de linóleo
y termitas en los muebles.
Después de cenar comida instantánea—
éramos tan nuevos en Norteamérica que esas
comidas nos parecían otro milagro de la tecnología—
Mamá visitaba a su amiga Hortencia,
una refugiada cubana tan gorda

que no podía caminar hasta nuestra casa
depués de un día de coser al destajo.
No teníamos televisor ni teléfono
así que me sentaba en la terraza,
observaba la autopista elevada
junto a nuestra casa y leía
novelas que me transportaban
lejos de Ybor City.

Los sábados en la tarde, caminaba
hasta la vieja biblioteca en el centro de Tampa
donde descubrí, en español,
La traición de Rita Hayworth de Manuel Puig.
Leía este libro en la noche
y durante los descansos en la fábrica:
una novela con un joven héroe homosexual
que me hacía soñar con musicales en tecnicolor de la
    MGM
y diosas en túnicas brillantes y ceñidas.
Yo era joven.

Sentado en el porche,
mientras la oscuridad se hacía profunda,
perforada por luciérnagas
estrellas fugaces que serpenteaban
entre los mangos;
yo soñaba con ciudades distantes,
ir a la universidad, escribir
libros, llevar una vida
que no tuviera nada que ver con una fábrica;
sin saber
que viajaría
lejos de Ybor City
exiliado del mundo de mi madre
y sin embargo sobreviviría.

Es sólo ahora, cuando evoco
al joven que era,
que puedo sentir
un dolor del alma por mi inocencia
por la fortaleza silenciosa de mi madre
por los miedos acallados,
por nuestras vidas que, aunque duras,
eran ricas en sueños.

Tumbling Through My Tumbaburro
by Jacinto Jesús Cardona

Tumbling through my tumbaburro,
I discover that to perturb is to cause a celestial body
to deviate from a theoretical regular orbital motion.

So I bounce my blue pelota down my street,
disturbing sleeping watchdogs.

I pass by a taquería and wave adiós to la tortillera
on break from her rolling pin duties.
She sits on a produce crate and basks in the aroma
de un cafecito con leche steaming in the nippy breeze.
She wipes her masa manos on her delantal,
her apron made from a flour sack, embroidered lace
on a Singer sewing machine.
I pass a faucet still reeling from an early freeze
and prepare to bounce my blue pelota down Buena
    Vista street, where I envision the
bushy black bigotes of unemployed machos and
    women who weep into their huipiles.

Calling All Chamacos!
by Jacinto Jesús Cardona

Chamacos!
Can you imagine standing in your black & white
      hightop
tenacos, your tenny shoes, and hearing those syllables
      for
the first time?

Chamaco?
You're talking to me?
Simón que sí. Eres un chamaco, un chavalón, a
      youngster, a kid. Chamaco. I like that.
Even Mack the Knife was a chamaco.

Chamaco.
I must admit de vez en cuando I was a depressed
      chamaco
hanging out in my lonely black & white tenacos
until the pump lights went out at the Shamrock filling
station. You would hear neither chus ni mus, not a sylla-
ble from my bilingual lips, my Tex-Mex lips. I would get
so depressed I would look up words of escape in my
Spanish-English deluxe lexicon. Under ch, fourth letter
of the Spanish alphabet, I discovered that in Central
America chamacos are called chapulínes, grasshop-
pers. If I were in the Dominican Republic, I would be a
chapulín wearing my chemulco, my woolen suit. In
Guatemala I could be a chapulín chiflando a los mangos melancólicos in my willow basket. Or I could be a
chapulín from Perú eating champuz, cornmeal mush
flavored with orange juice.

amor

love
by Gwylym Cano

there should be one hundred words for love
just as the peoples who have lived in snow so long
have so many words for snow. love
can be cold. difficult to walk on. slushy. mushy.
it will trick you. betray.
it can fall so silently on you that it mystifies—
soon everything is quiet
a blanket under which even the cold streets of your city
are warmed. clean. it can also sting.
invariably, it melts. often, then, it smells.
and each particle is different and you know no two
are the same, so never fear, lovely people, love comes
    again.

amor

por Gwylym Cano

translated from the English by Gwylym Cano

debería haber cien palabras para el amor
como los indígenas que viven con la nieve y
poseen tantas palabas para describirla. el amor
puede ser frío. difícil para caminar encima.
    blandengue.
resbaladizo. aayy! te va a engañar. traicionar.
puede caer tan silencioso que desconcierta
—de pronto, todo es tranquilo
una cobija en la cual se calientan hasta las calles frías
de tu ciudad. limpia. hasta puede picar.
invariablemente, se derrite. luego, frecuentemente,
    huele.
cada partícula es diferente y sabe—ninguna es
    parecida
a la otra, entonces, gente hermosa, nunca tenga
    miedo,
no es puro pedo, el amor vuelve otra vez.

Fill My World with Music
by Sandra María Esteves

Fill my world with music
sunrise and mint julep rhythm
    earthen melodies and congas quintiando
    I need to be harmonized
  so fill my crazy world with soft sounds
    a resonance   of graffiti melody
     a warm hand to touch
       simple things
 fill my stagnant world with vibration
in counterpoint
   till each finger of each hand on both arms
     is alive in my one entire body
  not one isolated beat
   or a flat note with no tone
  in some miscellaneous silence
I don't want to drown in Ay benditos!
   so please,
   fill me with something for real
   depend upon, set my walking time to
  I want some sound
to wake me up
   and work me out.

Llena mi mundo con música

por Sandra María Esteves

translated from the English by Isaac Goldemberg

Llena mi mundo con música
amaneceres y ritmo de hierbabuena
  melodías de barro y congas quintiando
  necesito que me armonicen
así que llena mi mundo loco con sonidos suaves
  una resonancia con melodías de graffiti
  una mano cálida para tocar
   cosas sencillas
llena mi mundo estancado con vibración
en contrapunto
  hasta que cada dedo de cada mano de mis dos brazos
  cobre vida en todo mi unico cuerpo
no un compás aislado
 o una nota desafinada sin tono
 en algún silencio misceláneo
no quiero ahogarme en Ay benditos!
 así que por favor,
 lléname con algo real
 depende de, pon mi hora de andar a
  quiero un sonido
que me despierte
  y me haga a vibrar.

Your Eyes
by Luis Alberto Ambroggio
translated from the Spanish by L. M. Carlson

Your eyes smile
invite
say everything
yes, maybe
eyes of honey, fire
they seduce
desire
punish
eyes green flowers
or white blossoms
they say
no, so-so
that you hurt
suffer
eyes of light, water
attract, defer
they follow
ignore
dance
open
look down
up
play with my eyes
with others
close in a cloud
divine eyes
bedeviled
they incite
betray
deceive

pardon
they are suns
fists of silver, onyx.

Your eyes wound
condemn
love
contain
and my eyes
like mirrors
mimic them.

Ocean eyes
black, green, red
imperious, timid
two stars
two howls.

Tus ojos
por Luis Alberto Ambroggio

Tus ojos
invitan
dicen todo
que sí o acaso
ojos de miel y fuego
seducen
quieren
castigan
ojos flores verdes
o azucenas
dicen que no
dicen que no a medias
que dueles
que sufres
ojos de luz y agua
de atracción y lejanía
siguen
ignoran
bailan
se abren
van abajo
arriba
con mis ojos juegan
con los otros
se cierran en una nube
ojos divinos
endemoniados
incitan
traicionan
engañan

perdonan
son soles
puñales de ónix y plata.

Tus ojos hieren
condenan
aman
contienen
y mis ojos
como espejos
los remedan.

Ojos océanos
negros, verdes, rojos
absolutos o menguados
de estrellas mutuas
y de mutuos llantos.

First Kiss
by Raquel Valle Senties

I stroll arm in arm with you
around Tampico's Plaza de Armas on a water-
heavy night. You are, Orlando, a walking cliché,
tall, dark and handsome in navy whites, speak
Portuguese. I don't. Our eyes roll,
eyebrows rise and hands fly like birds
in the feathery night. Your even teeth shine
like white mosaic tiles against skin weathered
by the sun and sea. Flecks of gold skim
in your brown eyes as they cling to mine. Fireflies,
tied to strings, sparkle on the necks of local
señoritas. We cross the street. Under the
shadowed embrace of the cathedral's arches,
your lips, sweet as a ripe fig, press mine.
From the plaza comes the faint sound
of the harp's hummingbird rhythms. It filters
through my pores like a movie sound track. I wait
for your arms to cradle my body. When they don't
I ask why. "Because I want to kiss you with my heart."

El primer beso

por Raquel Valle Sentíes

translated from the English by Raquel Valle Sentíes

Colgada de tu brazo, damos vueltas
en la Plaza de Armas en Tampico
en una noche pesada de humedad.
Tú, Orlando, eres un cliché andante,
alto, moreno y guapo en tu uniforme
blanco de marinero. Hablas sólo
portugués. Yo no. Nuestros ojos
dan vueltas, cejas suben y bajan
y manos vuelan como pájaros
en la noche emplumada. Tus dientes
parejos brillan como mosaicos blancos
contra tu piel curtida por el sol y el mar.
Puntos dorados destellan en tus ojos
café al unirse a los míos. Atados
a un hilo, cocuyos brillan en el cuello
de las chicas. Cruzamos la calle. Debajo
del abrazo oscuro de los arcos de la
catedral, tus labios, dulces como un higo
maduro, tocan los míos. De la plaza
viene el débil sonido de los ritmos del arpa.
Se filtra por mis poros como pista sonora
de película. Espero que tus brazos acunen
mi cuerpo. Al no hacerlo, te pregunto ¿por qué?
"Porque quiero besarte con el corazón."

El Parpadeo
by Trinidad Sánchez, Sr.

I
was writing you
a very, very round erotic poem
on the back of my eyelids in order
to make my movida, but it was lost,
the moment you raised your skirt
high enough for me to
take a second look . . .
and blink.

El parpadeo
por Trinidad Sánchez, Jr.
translated from the English by Isaac Goldemberg

Yo
te estaba escribiendo
un poema muy, muy redondo y erótico
detrás de mis párpados para
hacer mi movida, pero se perdió
en el momento que te alzaste la falda
lo bastante alto para yo
darte otra mirada . . .
y parpadear.

In Virginia Woods Near Leesburg
by Claudia Quiroz Cahill

Our fingers glowed cupping fireflies
near Leesburg.
Your long brown hair fell over lisps
of a fire.
Like so many nights before,
stories of love, and a flurry
of letters written to someone living
in a foreign city.
Then a sigh
came from the darkness
in the spruce boughs.

I lay on damp ground
scattered with leaf and mushroom,
and heard them stirring,
paws of a raccoon sweeping
a nightpath for a bite to eat.
When he was gone
I smelled his lingering fur,
my eyes took in
the unmenacing dark air, my fingers
touched his shining prints
left in an S swirl of earth.

I thought,
he must be crawling farther away,
scraping fallen trunks,
sniffing the grassy edges of a pond.
Wading through bristling vine,
under boughs and willows,
he comes upon a blackberry stem, then
clusters of ripe blackberries.

For the grizzly little hunter, they are
half-hidden secrets
discovered by pure accident.
Over my head, they are love blossoms
trickling in the dark.

En los bosques de Virginia
cerca de Leesburg
por Claudia Quiróz Cahill

translated from the English by Luis Alberto Ambroggio

Nuestros dedos relucían albergando luciérnagas
cerca de Leesburg.
Tu larga cabellera marrón cayó sobre los ceceos
de un fuego.
Como tantas noches antes,
historias de amor, y una oleada
de cartas escritas a alguien que vive
en una ciudad extranjera.
Luego un susurro
surgió de la oscuridad
en las ramas del abeto.

Yo acostada en tierra húmeda
esparcida con hoja y hongo,
escuché que se agitaban,
las zarpas de un mapache barriendo
un sendero nocturno hacia un bocado de comida.
Cuando él se fue
yo olí su piel persistente,
mis ojos capturaron
el inofensivo aire oscuro, mis dedos
tocaron sus huellas brillantes
dejadas en una S remolino de tierra.

Yo pensé
que estaría arrastrándose más lejos,
arañando troncos caidos,
olfateando los bordes de hierba de un estanque.
Escabulléndose a través de una zarza erizada,
bajo ramas y sauces,
encuentra un retoño de moras, luego
racimos de moras maduras.

Para el pequeño cazador gris, son
secretos apenas escondidos
descubiertos por pura casualidad.
Sobre mi cabeza, son pimpollos de amor
goteando en la oscuridad.

Prom Poem for Jorge Barroso
by Sandra M. Castillo

Even today, Jorge,
ten years after high school,
I think about it:
you sit with your sister Gisela
on Les' newly mowed grass,
far from the party that spreads
across the hilly lawn that would,
six years later, become the parking lot
for a lawyer's office.

New York dreams heavy on your shoulders,
you have come from band practice
to ask me to our senior prom.
You wear faded Levi's, white T-shirt, sneakers,
but Diane, my neighbor, our friend,
has imagined a pale-pink gown for herself.
She says she'd dance with you across
the tiled floor of the Doral with you
in a black tuxedo, a bow tie
the color of her dress
if I would let her, if I would say "No."

And it wasn't like the movies:
my football-player date wouldn't dance;
he ate all the food I didn't like
and didn't understand why I was silent, ashen.
I watched the women at our table huddle together,
away from their tuxedoed men,
from the Jim Beam they poured
into their transparent cups,
away from their pulsing laughter, their half-time.

I looked for you: your drummer hands,
your white-white teeth, your bow tie,
the color Diane envisioned,
seeing instead the ebb and flow
of long, bright dresses as they slowly rippled
under pale lights to form eddies of color.

Poema de baile de graduación
para Jorge Barroso
por Sandra M. Castillo

translated from the English by Carlos Aguasaco

Todavía hoy, Jorge,
diez años después de la secundaria,
pienso en ello:
sentado tú con tu hermana Gisela
en el césped recién cortado por Les
lejos de la fiesta que se extiende
a través del terreno ondulado que,
seis años después, se convertiría en un aparcadero
para una oficina de abogados.

Sueños neoyorkinos pesan en tus hombros,
has venido del ensayo de la banda
a invitarme al baile de graduación.
Vistes Levi's desteñidos, camiseta blanca, tenis,
pero Diane, mi vecina, nuestra amiga,
ha imaginado un vestido rosado claro para ella
       misma.
Dice que bailaría contigo a lo ancho
del salón del Doral, contigo
vestido con esmoquin negro, un corbatín
del color de su vestido
si yo la dejara, si dijera que "No."

Y no fue como en las películas:
el jugador de fútbol con quien fui no bailaba;
se comió toda la comida que no quise
y no comprendía por qué estaba callada, pálida.
Miré a las mujeres de nuestra mesa apiñarse,
lejos de sus hombres en esmoquin,
del Jim Beam que servían
en sus copas trasparentes,
lejos de su risa pulsante, su medio tiempo.

Te busqué: tus manos de percusionista,
tus dientes blancos-blancos, tu corbata,
el color que Diane imaginó,
Y vi, en cambio, el vaivén
de vestidos largos y brillantes que lentamente
       ondulaban
bajo las luces pálidas formando remolinos de colores.

Upon Knowing You
by Yeni Herrera

translated from the Spanish by L. M. Carlson

When I first met you
I feared loving you
And now that I have you
I fear losing you.

Al conocerte
por Yeni Herrera

Cuando te conocí
Tuve miedo de quererte
Ahora que te tengo
Tengo miedo de perderte.

Bilingual Love Poem
by José Antonio Burciaga
translated from the Spanish by L. M. Carlson

Your smile is un rayo de sol
picked
from your sonrisa
planted as a seed
within the sun
of my soul
with an ardiente passion
ardent pasión
sparking into tierra de fuego
where más is more
in a sea of sí
full of the salt of sal
in the saliva of saliva
making thirst
asking not to be first.
Two tongues that meet
make not a kiss
but bilingual love.

Poema de amor bilingüe
por José Antonio Burciaga

Tu sonrisa es un sunrise
cosechada
de tu smile
sembrada como una semilla
dentro del sol
de mi soul
con una ardent pasión
passion ardiente
chisporroteando en un mar de amar
donde more es amor
en un sea de sí
llena con la sal de salt
en la saliva de saliva
que da sed
pero jamás está sad.
Dos lenguas que se encuentran
no es un beso de boca
sino amor bilingüe.

family moments,
memories

Tía Chucha
by Luis J. Rodríguez

Every few years
Tía Chucha would visit the family
in a tornado of song
and open us up
as if we were an overripe avocado.
She was a dumpy, black-haired
creature of upheaval
who often came unannounced
with a bag of presents,
including homemade perfumes and colognes
that smelled something like
rotting fish
on a hot day at the tuna cannery.

They said she was crazy.
Oh sure, she once ran out naked
to catch the postman
with a letter that didn't belong to us.
I mean, she had this annoying habit
of boarding city buses
and singing at the top of her voice
(one bus driver even refused to go on
until she got off).
But crazy?

To me, she was the wisp
of the wind's freedom,
a music-maker
who once tried to teach me guitar
but ended up singing

and singing
me listening,
and her singing
until I put the instrument down
and watched the clock
click the lesson time away.

I didn't learn guitar,
but I learned something
about her craving
for the new, the unbroken
. . . so she could break it.
Periodically she banished
herself from the family
and was the better for it.

I secretly admired Tía Chucha.
She was always quick with a story,
another "Pepito" joke
or a handwritten lyric
that she would produce
regardless of the occasion.

She was a despot
of desire,
uncontainable
as a splash of water
on a varnished table.

I wanted to remove
the layers
of unnatural seeing,
the way Tía Chucha beheld
the world, with first eyes,

like an infant
who can discern
the elixir
within milk.

I wanted to be
one of the prizes
she stuffed into
her rumpled bag.

Tía Chucha

por Luis J. Rodríguez

translated from the English by Carlos Aguasaco

De vez en cuando
Tía Chucha visitaba la familia
canción-huracán
que nos abrió como si fuéramos aguacates maduros
regordeta, pelinegra
criatura de convulsión
que a menudo venía sin anunciarse,
con una bolsa de regalos
que incluían perfumes hechos en casa y colonias
que olían como
pescado pudriéndose
en un día caluroso en la empacadora de atún.

Decían que estaba loca.
Pues, una vez salió a correr desnuda
para alcanzar al cartero
con una carta que no nos pertenecía.
Quiero decir, que tenía el hábito irritante
de abordar los autobuses
y cantar con todas sus fuerzas
(incluso hubo un chofer que se rehusó a continuar
hasta que ella se bajó).
¿Pero loca?

Para mí, ella era un jirón
de la libertad del viento,
una hacedora de música
que una vez trató de enseñarme a tocar guitarra
pero terminó cantando
y cantando

y yo escuchando,
y ella cantando
hasta que bajé el instrumento
y vi el tic-tac del reloj
llevarse el tiempo de la clase.

No aprendí a tocar guitarra,
pero aprendí algo sobre sus ansias
por lo nuevo, lo compuesto
. . . lo que ella podía descomponer.
Periódicamente ella misma
se desterraba de la familia
y era la mejor por ello.

Yo admiraba secretamente a Tía Chucha.
Siempre estaba lista con un cuento,
otro chiste de "Pepito"
o un poema escrito a mano
que producía
sin importar la ocasión.

Era una déspota
del deseo,
incontenible
como agua salpicada
en una mesa barnizada.

Yo quería remover
las capas
de apariencia artificial,
la manera en que Tía Chucha contemplaba
el mundo, con sus ojos infantiles,

como un bebé
que puede apreciar
el elixir
en la leche.

Deseaba ser
uno de los premios
que ella atesoraba
en su bolsa arrugada.

Martin and My Father
by David Hernandez

Martin was too peaceful for me.
He let those Deep-South dogs bite him
Police club his head
Cowards bomb his house
Firemen hose him down
and judges throw him in jail.

I used to pack a 357 Magnum
and if anybody messed with me,
I would aim, pull the trigger
and feel the kick of the gun
saturated in spic anger.
I wanted to kill all the
racist pigs in the world
and marching peacefully
like Martin did, wasn't
about to do it.

One time while arguing with my father
I pulled a knife on him.
That night he cried himself to sleep
and I felt like an assassin.
The next day I heard that Martin
was shot dead and my heart crumbled
for him and my father.

My anger turned ice-blue hot,
well-kept, on target,
proportionately forever and
it was on this anvil that
my pen was forged.

So I took my gun and knife,
threw them in the lake
and watched them drown.
Then I went home and while
my father took a nap on the couch
with the TV blaring
about Martin's death,
I kissed him with a poem.

And I'll tell you,
 That Martin,
      He was something else.

Martin y mi padre

por David Hernandez

translated from the English by Carlos Aguasaco

Martin era demasiado pacífico para mi gusto.
Dejaba que esos perros del profundo sur lo mordieran,
la policía le apaleara la cabeza,
los cobardes bombardearan su casa,
los bomberos lo empaparan,
y los jueces lo echaran a la cárcel.

Yo solía llevar conmigo una Magnum 357
y si alguien llegara a molestarme
le apuntaría, halaría el gatillo
y sentiría el retroceso de la pistola
saturado de rabia de spic.
Quería matar a todos
los cerdos racistas del mundo
y marchando pacíficamente, como lo hizo Martin,
no iba a lograrlo.

Alguna vez mientras discutí con mi padre
le esgrimí un cuchillo.
Esa noche mi padre lloró hasta dormirse
y yo me sentí como un asesino.
El día siguiente oí que Martin
había muerto abaleado y mi corazón se desmoronó
por él y por mi padre.

Mi rabia se volvió de color azul frío e hiviente,
bien resguardada, enfocada,
para siempre proporcionada y
fue sobre este yunque
que se forjó mi pluma.

Así que tomé mi cuchillo y mi pistola,
los arrojé al lago
y los vi hundirse.
Luego fui a casa y
mientras mi padre tomaba una siesta en el sofá
con la tele pregonando
la muerte de Martin,
lo besé con un poema.

Y te diré,
  Ese Martin,
      era un caso aparte.

Dead Pig's Revenge
by Michele Serros

I knew every time
Dad packed us up
to travel the distance
from Oxnard to Chino
my family would eat good.
We would eat free
'cuz fave uncle Vincent
was a restaurateur,
a professional businessman,
proud owner of
a catering truck.
A coach as in
Super-rico taco
mariachi blaring
expired license plates
lonchería,
but a nice one.

He always dreamed of
one day owning his own business,
becoming a self-employed man,
his own boss,
soccer on Sundays,
sleeping off hangovers
on Monday.
He loved those short workweeks.
So finally after scraping up
what little money he had,
he got the coach.
It helped Johnny,

his fourth kid, get through college,
kept Aunt Dolly up all night,
chopping
and chopping,
cilantro,
onions,
tomatoes,
with dull knives.
His place had everything
any fine establishment had:
sesos,
lenguas,
tripas
and my favorite
chicharrones.

My mother always warned:
"That's solid lard,
pure grease.
That poor dead pig's
gonna have revenge on you yet,
make you fat,
make you fart,
scatter your skin with
white-tipped pimples.
No man's gonna want you."
Her weak threats
didn't work.
Man, couldn't get enough
of that crackly pork skin.
I crammed them in tortillas
that were always too small,
so I ate them right out of the pot,
throwing small crispy bits into the air,

like popcorn
letting them land
in my open anxious mouth.
I used to eye
my cousin Amy's pet piglet.
With a wink I'd say,
"See you in a couple of years . . .
in my belly!"
That'd send Amy crying into the house.

One ordinary visit
while I sat in the coach's shade
I could see my father
talking chickens with Uncle Vincent,
my mother inside with Aunt Dolly.
I was shoving my dear chicharrones
into my mouth.
Something happened.
They stayed right there,
in my throat.
I swallowed hard to help them down,
coughed firmly to help them up,
but they wouldn't budge.
I could feel coarse pig hairs
tickle my throat,
but I wasn't laughing.
This was not funny.
I couldn't breathe.
I was going to DIE!
My mother was right,
the dead pig's revenge!
I was going to DIE.

My father
was suddenly miles away . . .
Thoughts raced through my mind,
Who'll take care of Miss Rosie,
my pet goat?
Still haven't got "Student of the Month."
But more agonizing than
any of these things,
than any of this,
I thought of the headline,
the headline in my obituary:

Chicharrones Choke Chicana Child to Death (in Chino)

Oh my God,
I couldn't die with a headline like that!
The humiliation.
I didn't want to die.
I wanted to live!
I wanted to live!
My legs lost balance . . .
Suddenly a thud.
It was dark.

I woke up to find
Cousin Amy above me.
"You were turning blue,
so I punched you on the back
like they do on TV."
That night Amy got her favorite dinner.
My mom and dad
shook their heads in disgust,
hearing her repeat the story
over and over again.

But I didn't care,
I was alive!
I was free!
to walk,
to breathe,
to think,
to eat.
I stepped out to the backyard
walked over to the caged pen
to watch over Amy's sleeping piglet.
It was so full of life
a beautiful breathing thing
I spent all night with it.
Watching,
thinking,
waiting,
        salivating.

La venganza del chancho muerto
por Michele Serros

translated from the English by Carlos Aguasaco

Yo sabía que cada vez
que mi padre nos empacaba
para viajar la distancia
entre Oxnard y Chino
mi familia comería bien.
Comeríamos gratis
porque mi tío favorito, Vincent
era un restaurantero,
todo un hombre de negocios,
orgulloso propietario de
un camión restaurante.
Una vagoneta como esas de
tacos super-ricos
música de mariachi retumbando
placas suspendidas
lonchería,
pero linda.

Siempre soñó
con tener su propio negocio algún día,
volverse un trabajador independiente,
su propio jefe,
fútbol los domingos,
dormir las resacas
el lunes.
Amaba las semanas de trabajo cortas.
Así que después de reunir a duras penas
el poco dinero que tenía,
compró la vagoneta.
Esto ayudó a Johnny,

su cuarto hijo, a costearse la universidad,
mantenía a Tía Dolly desvelada,
picando
y picando,
cilantro,
cebolla,
tomates,
con cuchillos desafilados.
Su negocio tenía todo
lo que cualquier buen establecimiento tenía:
sesos,
lenguas,
tripas,
y mi plato favorito
chicharrones.

Mi madre siempre me lo advirtió:
"Eso es manteca sólida,
pura grasa.
Ese pobre chancho muerto
se va a vengar de ti,
te engordará,
te hará echar pedos,
te cubrirá la piel
con espinillas.
Ningún hombre se va a interesar en ti."
Sus débiles amenazas
no funcionaron.
Hombre, no podía saciarme
de esos chicharrones crujientes.
Los atiborraba en tortillas
que siempre se quedaban demasiado pequeñas,
así que los comía directamente de la sartén,
que lanzaba pequeños bocados crujientes por el aire,

como palomitas de maíz
dejándolos aterrizar
en mi abierta y ansiosa boca.
Solía mirar
el cerdito que mi prima Amy tenía de mascota.
Con un guiño le decía,
"¡Te veo en un par de años . . .
en mi panza!"
Esto enviaba a Amy llorando a su casa.

En una visita ordinaria
mientras estaba sentada bajo el parasol de la vagoneta
podía ver a mi padre
hablando de pollos con mi Tío Vincent,
mi madre estaba adentro con Tía Dolly.
Yo me estaba embutiendo mis queridos chicharrones
en la boca.
Algo sucedió.
Se quedaron allí mismo,
en mi garganta.
Traté de tragar fuerte para ayudarlos a bajar,
tosí firmemente para expulsarlos,
pero no se movían.
Podía sentir los ásperos pelos de cerdo
haciéndome cosquillas en la garganta,
pero no me hacían reir.
Esto no era gracioso.
No podía respirar.
¡Me iba a MORIR!
¡Mi madre tenía razón,
la venganza del chancho muerto!
Me iba a MORIR.

Mi padre
de repente estaba a millas de distancia . . .
Muchos pensamientos pasaron por mi mente,
¿quién cuidaría a la señorita Rosie,
mi cabra mascota?
Aún no me habían nombrado "estudiante del mes."
Pero más angustiante que
todas estas cosas,
que cualquiera de estas cosas,
era pensar en el titular,
el titular de mi obituario:

Chicharrones sofocan a una niñita chicana hasta
causarle la muerte (en Chino)

¡Ay Dios mío,
no podía morir con un titular como ese!
La humillación.
No quería morir.
¡Quería vivir!
¡Quería vivir!
Mis piernas perdieron el equilibrio . . .
Un golpe sordo de repente.
Todo estaba oscuro.

Me desperté y encontré
a mi prima Amy sobre mi.
"Te estabas poniendo azul,
así que te golpeé la espalda
como hacen en la tele."
Esa noche Amy tuvo su comida favorita.
Mi mami y mi papi
movían sus cabezas en señal de disgusto,
mientras la escuchaban repetir la historia

una y otra vez.
Pero no me importaba,
¡Estaba viva!
¡Era libre!
para caminar,
respirar,
pensar,
comer.
Salí al patio,
caminé hasta el corral
para vigilar el cerdito dormido de Amy.
Estaba tan lleno de vida,
un hermoso ser vivo,
pasé toda la noche con él.
Observando,
pensando,
esperando,
      con la boca hecha agua.

At a Peach Orchard in Virginia
by Claudia Quiróz Cahill

Against an orchard of
peach trees and sprouting grass,
overripe bellies released
their heavy peach smells.
A stranger pulled a peach from its stem,
then ate it
as if it were the last one
in the world. So much
in this world goes unnoticed,
where shapely blossoms burst, then
drop to the ground.

An old man approached us
on a tractor. His eyes gazed down
at our empty crate.
He looked hard
at the crate and at us. He said
we didn't pick the peaches before
our picnic; we had to leave the grounds.

My mother's eyes squinted
under the sun. Stay calm
I told her.
Aunt Bachi who spoke no English
whispered ¿por qué hermana, por qué?

Passing FRESH PEACHES hand-painted
across planks, passing gas stations
and cornfields stretching to wild tangles,
the family picnic
became a vivid memory for the children,
prejudice
wiped away like
warm breath over a car window.

En una granja de duraznos en Virginia
por Claudia Quiróz Cahill

translated from the English by Carlos Aguasaco

Junto a una granja de
árboles de duraznos y césped creciente,
las panzas maduras liberaban
su fuerte olor a durazno.
Un extraño arrancó un durazno de su tallo,
luego lo comió
como si fuera el último
en el mundo. Tantas cosas
pasan inadvertidas en este mundo,
donde las flores más bellas revientan y
caen al suelo.

Un viejo se nos acercó en un tractor.
Sus ojos contemplaban
nuestro canasto vacío.
Miraba firmemente
el canasto y a nosotros. Dijo que
no escogimos los duraznos antes
de nuestro picnic; que teníamos que dejar esas tierras.

Los ojos de mi madre se entornaron
bajo el sol. Cálmate
le dije.
Tía Bachi que no hablaba inglés
susurró ¿por qué hermana, por qué?

Al pasar frente a DURAZNOS FRESCOS pintados a
    mano
sobre vallas de madera, por gasolineras
y campos de maíz que se estiran en marañas,
el picnic familiar
se convirtió en un recuerdo vívido para los niños,
el prejuicio
se esfumó como
el aliento tibio en la ventana de un auto.

The Piñata Painted with a Face Like Mine
by Martín Espada

I was in the basement when my brother came home
without a shirt covering his hungry chest.
He saw a fight by the river,
eight-track tapes stolen from somebody's car,
a broken bottle jammed in the armpit
and blood shooting out, so that even my brother's shirt
wrapped around the wound
did not keep the startled boy from dying.
That summer my brother stayed by the river,
passing the lukewarm wine or a pipe of hashish,
bragging about refrigerators of meat
plundered in unguarded garages.

I saw him slip the bills from my father's wallet
into his pants. When I told my brother this,
he promised a kitchen knife
plunged between my ribs as I slept.
"Go get it," I said. When he turned
to the kitchen, a wave of blood crashed
in the chambers of my forehead.
Too quickly, my knuckles in his hair, his skull
thudding off the wall. I wanted to see
the blood irrigating the folds of his brain;
I wanted to break this piñata
painted with a face like mine.

Only amazement could have stopped me.
Amazing was the sight of my father's face.
He stood before us, a man with hands
forbidding as tarantulas, and cried.

After twenty years, one brother cannot sleep
waiting for the other. I wait for him,
the cool knife sliding against my skin.
And he waits for me, my knuckles in his hair,
to finish cracking open the piñata
painted with a face like mine.

La piñata pintada con una cara como la mía

por Martín Espada

translated from the English by Carlos Aguasaco

Yo estaba en el sótano cuando mi hermano llegó a
    casa
sin una camisa que cubriera su pecho hambriento.
Él vio una pelea cerca del río,
cintas eight-track robadas del auto de alguien,
una botella rota atascada en la axila
y sangre derramándose tanto que incluso la camisa de
    mi hermano
envuelta alrededor de la herida
no evitó que el angustiado chico muriera.
Ese verano mi hermano se quedó cerca del río,
pasando vino tibio o una pipa de hachís,
jactándose de refrigeradores de carne
saqueados en garajes sin vigilancia.

Lo vi sacar los billetes de la cartera de mi padre
y deslizarlos entre sus pantalones. Cuando se lo dije,
me prometió el cuchillo de la cocina
hundido entre mis costillas mientras dormía.
"Tráelo," le dije. Cuando giró
hacia la cocina, una oleada de sangre estalló
en el interior de mi frente.
Muy rápido, mis nudillos en su pelo, su cráneo
golpeándo contra el muro. Yo quería ver
la sangre irrigando los pliegues de su cerebro;
quería romper esta piñata
pintada con una cara como la mía.

Sólo el asombro pudo haberme detenido.
Asombrosa era la expresión en el rostro de mi padre.
Se paró junto a nosotros, un hombre con manos
amenazantes como tarántulas, y lloró.

Después de veinte años, un hermano no puede dormir
aguardando por el otro. Yo lo espero,
su cuchillo frío deslizándose contra mi piel.
Y él me espera, mis nudillos en su pelo,
para terminar de reventar la piñata
pintada con una cara como la mía.

Saturdays Set Within Memory
by Isaac Goldemberg
translated from the Spanish by L. M. Carlson

Saturdays set within memory
Kids in the neighborhood
    delivering bread
and the prayer cut short
The house settles down like a word falls quiet
Gracious grandma rests in the shadows
    a relic
My vigilant father prays with the voice of
    a patriarch
My mother lights the oven
    (still time)
She kneads our bread with her silences

Sábado aferrado a la memoria
por Isaac Goldemberg

Sábado aferrado a la memoria
Han corrido los muchachos del barrio a repartirse
    el pan y se ha cortado la oración
La casa se hunde como una palabra en silencio
La hospitalaria abuela reposa en la penumbra
    como un ídolo
Mi padre reza con su voz de patriarca y centinela
Mi madre enciende el horno
    (aún queda tiempo)
Amasa nuestro pan con sus silencios

This Is for Mamacita
by Willie Perdomo

too tired
for words

you say
give me life

I
love you

like always
I return all

the kisses you blow
my way

I can see
dry tears

left in your
sunken cheeks

I have heard
you cry

twice today
once when the sun

came out and Carlitos
didn't give you

the ten dollars
he promised you

upon awakening
and then you cried

real tears when
one of the boys

gave Machito five dollars
if he dared to ask you

to suck his
those were real tears

I saw you too tired
to say a thing

I say give me life
I love you

when you return
all the kisses

I blow
your way

Esto es para mamacita
por Willie Perdomo

translated from the English by Mayra Santos Febres
and Rafael Franco

demasiada cansada
para las palabras

me dices
dame vida

yo
te amo

como siempre
te devuelvo todos

los besos que soplas
en mi camino

puedo ver
lágrimas secas

al fondo
de tus mejillas hundidas

yo te he
escuchado llorar

dos veces hoy
una cuando salió el sol

y Carlitos
no te dio

los diez pesos
que te prometió

cuando despertaras
y después lloraste

lágrimas de verdad cuando
uno de los muchachos

le dio a Machito cinco dólares
si se atrevía a pedirte

que se lo mamaras
aquellas eran lágrimas verdaderas

te vi demasiado cansada
para decir algo

yo digo dame vida
te amo

cuando me devuelves
todos los besos

que soplo
en tu camino

victory

Triumph

by Marjorie Agosín

translated from the Spanish by L. M. Carlson

Triumph is not ascending golden stairs
nor collecting various crowns
but understanding that the most diminutive flowers
  grow
in the desert
recognizing them
knowing their small magnificence

Triumph is a word dressed right
a world without crowns graced with stars

El triunfo
por Marjorie Agosín

El triunfo no es ascender por las escaleras
doradas
ni obtener coronas dispersas
es entender a las flores diminutas que crecen
en el desierto
reconocerlas,
saberlas grandiosas en su pequeñez

El triunfo es una palabra vestida de gracia
un mundo sin coronas tan sólo con estrellas

In a Minute
by Robert B. Feliciano

In a minute
a world could end
yet I strive to live and stay alive
Each day is
an adventure in the worst weather
In a minute
two people fall in love
Or shove one another aside as the daytime
sky slides to the west
In a minute
anything could happen
A minute is
all I need to keep alive
and above the knees

En un minuto

por Robert B. Feliciano

translated from the English by L. M. Carlson

En un minuto
un mundo podría estallar
sin embargo anhelo vivir y quedarme vivo
Cada día es
una aventura en el clima más desagradable
En un minuto
dos personas se enamoran
O se empujan uno al otro a un costado
como el cielo soleado
resbala al oeste
En un minuto
cualquier cosa podría pasar
Un minuto es
todo lo que necesito para quedarme vivo
y de pie

Piece by Piece

by Luis J. Rodríguez

Piece by piece
They tear at you:
Peeling away layers of being,
Lying about who you are,
Speaking for your dreams.

In the squalor of their eyes
You are an outlaw.
Dressing you in a jacket of lies
tailor made in steel
You fit their perfect picture.

Take it off!
Make your own mantle.
Question the interrogators.
Eyeball the death in their gaze.
Say you won't succumb.
Say you won't believe them
When they rename you.
Say you won't accept their codes,
Their colors, their putrid morals.

Here you have a way.
Here you can sing victory.
Here you are not a conquered race
Perpetual victim
The sullen face in a thunderstorm.

Hands/mind, they are carving out
A sanctuary.
Use these weapons against them.
Use your given gifts—
They are not stone.

Pedazo a pedazo

por Luis J. Rodríguez

translated from the English by Carlos Aguasaco

Pedazo a pedazo
Te desgarran:
Arrancando capas del ser,
Mintiendo acerca de quién eres,
Hablando por tus sueños.

En la inmundicia de sus ojos
Eres un proscrito.
Vestido con una chaqueta de mentiras
hecha a la medida con acero
Encajas en su fotografía perfecta.

¡Quítatela!
Haz tu propio manto.
Interroga a los interrogadores.
Encara a la muerte en su mirada.
Di que no sucumbirás.
Di que no vas a creerles
Cuando cambien tu nombre.
Di que no aceptarás sus códigos,
Sus colores, sus morales pútridas.

Aquí tienes un camino.
Aquí puedes cantar victoria.
Aquí no eres una raza conquistada
Víctima perpetua
El rostro hosco en la tormenta.

Manos/mente, están esculpiendo
Un santuario.
Usa estas armas en su contra.
Usa lo que te ha sido dado—
Ellos no son de piedra.

Ode to the Tortilla
by Gina Valdés

translated from the Spanish by Gina Valdés

Daily I say, pass me a tortilla
as if saying, pass me the sun
the moon, kiss me

Round blessing, our daily tlayuda
our sacred tlaxcalli

Spoon of seamstresses, meat of bricklayers
inspiration of carpenters, bread of the unemployed

¡Santa Tortilla de cada día!
I long for your tasty company

Child of the golden seed stolen back from hell
by Quetzalcóatl
so we can persist on earth
taste heaven

Hard little seed of generosity, daughter of Chicomecóatl
you bathe in lime, soak, swell, shed your hardness
        for us
You roll with metate and molcajete
those volcanoes

The magic chanting of hands shapes your full moon
        face
the comal kisses you hotly on both cheeks
prepares you for my mouthful of kisses

If we become what we most desire
next life I may be born a tortilla

to bless with my smoky scent
someone who loves me

Daily I say, pass me a tortilla
edible sun, nutritious moon
earthly host, planetary delight
I want to celebrate
my body of corn, this gold light
that circles my spirit

Oda a la tortilla
por Gina Valdés

A diario digo, pásame una tortilla
como quien dice, pásame el sol
la luna, bésame

Bendición redonda, nuestra tlayuda diaria
nuestra tlaxcalli sagrada

Cuchara de costureras, carne de albañiles
inspiración de carpinteros, pan de los desempleados

¡Santa Tortilla de cada día!
Añoro tu sabrosa compañía

Hija de la semilla dorada rescatada del infierno
por Quetzalcóatl
para que podamos persistir en la tierra
probar el cielo

Dura semilla generosa, hija de Chicomecóatl
te bañas en agua de cal, te remojas, te hinchas
te despojas de tu dureza por nosotros
das vueltas en metate y molcajete
esos volcanes

El cantar mágico de las manos moldean tu cara
de luna llena, el comal te besa ardientemente
en las dos mejillas, preparándote para mi boca
llena de besos

Si nos convertimos en lo que más deseamos
en la siguiente vida quizá yo sea tortilla

para bendecir con mi humeante fragancia
a quien me ame

A diario digo, pásame una tortilla
sol comestible, luna nutritiva
hostia terrestre, delicia planetaria
para celebrar
mi cuerpo de maíz, esta luz de oro
que circunda mi espíritu

The Journey That We Are

by Luis Alberto Ambroggio

translated from the Spanish by L. M. Carlson

Your mystery holds
the "where do I come from"
and the "where am I going"
with the infinite path
of destiny.

Like a plane
you can
make and unmake heights foot by foot.
You are
bird on a unique flight.
You are
petal on a blessed wind.
And it is possible to keep strong
like the sun
with a fire in your heart.

El viaje que somos
por Luis Alberto Ambroggio

Tu misterio acuna
el "de dónde vengo"
y el "a dónde voy"
con el camino infinito
de la distancia.

Es posible como avión
hacer y deshacer la altura metro a metro.
Pájaro de un único vuelo.
Pétalo en un viento endiosado.
Es posible rejuvenecer
como el sol con un corazón de fuego.

Look to the Sun
by Sandra María Esteves

Look to the sun
  as it comes
every morning

look to the sun
  every day

see how it flows
on the river
  it sparkles

see how it glows
  in your eyes

feel how it softly
warms all your fingers

feel how it warms
all your heart

look to the sun
  rising high
    every day

Look to the sun.

Mira al sol
por Sandra María Esteves
translated from the English by Carlos Aguasaco

Mira al sol
  como viene
cada mañana

mira al sol
  cada día

mira como fluye
destella
 en el río

mira como resplandece
  en tus ojos

siente como entibia
todos tus dedos

siente como calienta
todo tu corazón

mira al sol
  que se eleva hacia lo alto
    cada día

Mira al sol.

For Bert Corona
by Trinidad Sánchez, Sr.

Te oigo mi hermano,
te acompaño en tu canto
formando justicia.
Bien que lo sabes—
it will take more than the river
to divide our brown canela colors
which give us strength,
it will take more than the mountains
to separate nuestra sangre
which gives us life,
it will take more than the desert's heat
to dry our thirst for justice,
it will take more than link fences
to fragment our sueños
de tanta raza nueva!
It will take more than English
for us to forget who we are!
Somos de la misma tierra
el mismo sol nos quema
la misma lluvia da la vida
al maíz/frijol sembrado.
Te oigo mi hermano—
as long as there is breath
cantamos las canciones nuevas,
con el arco iris a nuestra espalda,
seguimos organizando
a un futuro liberado!

glossary

language, identity

"SPANISH"

¡Abuela, / Teléfono! Una vendedora / De: Grandmother, /
Telephone! A seller / Of
¡Ay, Dios!: Oh, God!
¡Chihuahua!: an expression of amazement used by Mexicans,
as in "wow!"
abuelo: grandfather
compa: abbreviated form of *compadre,* meaning "buddy" or
"my bro"
Chicharrones: a snack made of crispy pork rinds or pork
cracklings
mami: mommy
papi: poppy
flor: flower
cocos: coconuts
gato: cat
perro: dog

"I AM FROM QUISQUELLA LA BELLA"

Quisquella la bella: Quisquella (town) the beautiful
bachata: a party
perico ripiao: telephone calling card

Dios: God
patria: country
libertad: freedom
pernil: roast pork
plátanos: plantains

"THE HANDS"

requintos: small guitars
güiros: percussion instruments made from dried gourds
claves: percussion instruments used in the Antilles
timbales: kettledrums
charangos: five-string guitars
guitarrones: four- or five-string bass guitars
tin tin timbaleo tingo: fanciful musical onomatopoeia
rumbeando: moving in a certain direction
albóndigas: meatballs

"I AM WHO I AM, SO WHAT"

huapangos: a popular folkloric dance in Mexico (plural)
rancheras: ranch songs with typically straightforward lyrics
"Las mañanitas": "The Sweet Mornings," a popular Mexican song
pocha: an Americanized Mexican

"MY GRADUATION SPEECH"

ponce: a town in the southern part of Puerto Rico
mayagüez: a town on the west coast of Puerto Rico
carolina: a town on the north coast of Puerto Rico, next to San Juan
tengo las venas aculturadas: my veins have adapted to another culture
escribo en spanglish: I write in spanglish

tato: sir
tonto: stupid
si me fui ya: if I've already gone
si me dicen barranquitas: if they tell me Barranquitas (town in Puerto Rico)
¿con qué se come eso?: what do you eat that with?
si me dicen caviar: if they tell me caviar
digo: I say
ahí supe que estoy jodío: there, I knew I'm screwed
ahí supe que estamos jodíos: there, I knew we are all screwed
hablo lo inglés matao: I speak a mutilated English
no sé leer ninguno bien: I don't know how to read either well
¡ay, virgen, yo no sé hablar!: Oh, Virgin, I don't know how to speak!

neighborhoods

"ARMITAGE STREET"

Don: a title indicating respect or erudition

"TUMBLING THROUGH MY TUMBABURRO"

tumbaburro: Mexicanism for dictionary
pelota: ball
taquería: a food shop that sells tacos
adiós: good-bye
tortillera: a woman who makes tortillas
cafecito con leche: a cup of coffee with milk
masa manos: dough hands
delantal: apron

bigotes: mustaches
huipiles: a kind of loose blouse, often woven, worn by women in Mexico, Guatemala, and Honduras (plural)

"CALLING ALL CHAMACOS!"

chamaco: Mexican slang for boy
tenacos: tennis shoes
Simón que sí: Of course
Eres un chamaco, un chavalón: You're a kid, a young man
de vez en cuando: sometimes
chus ni mus: not a word
chapulín chiflando a los mangos melancólicos: kid making fun of sad-looking mangoes

amor

"LOVE"

no es puro pedo: it's not malarkey (or not a fantasy)

"FILL MY WORLD WITH MUSIC"

quintiando: guitar strumming
¡Ay, benditos!: Common Puerto Rican expression meaning "oh, my goodness!"

"EL PARPADEO"

el parpadeo: winking or blinking
movida: move, as in "to make my move"

family moments, memories

"TÍA CHUCHA"

Pepito: popular type of joke referred to by the name Pepe

"DEAD PIG'S REVENGE"

Super-rico taco: super-delicious taco
lonchería: a place that serves lunches
sesos: brains
lenguas: tongues
tripas: intestines, also known as tripe

victory

"ODE TO THE TORTILLA"

tlayuda: Indian name for the corn tortilla
tlaxcalli: Indian name for the corn tortilla
Quetzalcóatl: Aztec god of peace and culture
Chicomecóatl: Aztec goddess of hard corn
metate: square stone used in Mexico to grind corn
molcajete: stone or clay mortar
comal: clay disc used to cook tortillas

"FOR BERT CORONA"

Te oigo mi hermano: I hear you my brother
te acompaño en tu canto: I join you in your song
formando justicia: creating justice
Bien que lo sabes: you know very well
canela: cinnamon
nuestra sangre: our blood
sueños: dreams

de tanta raza nueva: of this new race
Somos de la misma tierra: We are of the same land
el mismo sol nos quema: the same sun burns us
la misma lluvia da la vida: the same rain gives life
al maíz/frijol sembrado: corn/bean planted
cantamos las canciones nuevas: we'll sing new songs
con el arco iris a nuestra espalda: with a rainbow at our back
seguimos organizando: we'll continue organizing
un futuro liberado: a liberated future

biographical notes

Marjorie Agosín was born in Chile. She is currently a professor of Spanish at Wellesley College and has received many awards, including the United Nations Leadership Award in Human Rights. She has published more than twenty books of poetry, as well as eight memoirs and six books of fiction. Among her poetry volumes are *At the Threshold of Memory*, *Dear Anne Frank*, *Las chicas desobedientes*, and *Conchalí*.

Carlos Aguasaco was born in Bogotá, Colombia. An essayist, poet, and literary critic, he has written a book of poetry entitled *Conversando con el angel*. He currently lives in New York City, where he teaches high school and also works as an adjunct professor at the Center for Worker Education at City College.

Ivette Álvarez is a student in the New York City public school system. She has published her poetry in the anthology *Streams 8*.

Luis Alberto Ambroggio was born in Córdoba, Argentina, but has lived in the United States since 1967. A prolific writer of poetry, he has published many books, including *El testigo se desnuda*, *Hombre del aire*, *Oda ensimismada*, and *Los habitantes del poeta*. He also writes theater reviews. He currently lives in Virginia.

Kizzilie Bonilla is a student in the New York City public school system. She has published her poetry in the anthology *Streams 9*.

José Antonio Burciaga was a poet, short story writer, essayist, and painter who died in 1996. Among his best-known works are *Drink Culture* and *Amor indocumentado*. He was a leading figure in the Chicano literary and artistic movement.

Claudia Quiróz Cahill, a poet of Bolivian parentage, holds an M.F.A. in creative writing from Columbia University. Her poetry has appeared in several magazines, including *River Styx* and *Antaeus,* and in the anthology *Cool Salsa*. She resides in Virginia.

Gwylym Cano is a poet who lives in Denver, Colorado. He holds a James Ryan Morris Tombstone Award for Poetry. He also acts, having worked with El Centro Su Teatro, the Bilingual Foundation for the Arts, and Floricanto U.S.A. Mr. Cano owns and operates his own independent film company, Fool Moon Productions. He says he is "the world's only living Welsh-Xicano."

Jacinto Jesús Cardona was born in Palacios, Texas, but grew up in Alice, the hub of South Texas. He teaches English at Palo Alto College and at the Trinity University Upward Bound Program in San Antonio, Texas. He is the author of the poetry volume *Pan Dulce* and has read his verse on National Public Radio and PBS television.

Lori Marie Carlson holds an M.A. in Hispanic literature from Indiana University. She is the author of nine books for young adults and children including the acclaimed *Cool Salsa* and *American Eyes*. She has also written two novels, *The Sunday Tertulia* and *The Flamboyant*. She lives in New York City.

Sandra M. Castillo was born in Havana, Cuba. She fled the island with her family in 1970 on one of the last of President Johnson's Freedom Flights. In addition to having written books of poetry, among them *Red Letters* and *My Father Sings, to My Embarrassment*, she teaches English at Miami Dade Community College.

Martín Espada, a poet and educator, was born in Brooklyn. Among his books of poetry are *Alabanza, City of Coughing and Dead Radiators, Imagine the Angels of Bread*, and *A Mayan Astronomer in Hell's Kitchen*. He is an associate professor of English at the University of Massachusetts-Amherst.

Sandra María Esteves, one of the better-known exponents of the Nuyorican literary movement, is the author of six published collections of poetry, among them *Finding Your Way, Yerba buena, Undelivered Love Poems* and *Bluestown Mockingbird Mambo*. A performance poet of Dominican and Puerto Rican heritage, she began writing in the 1970s.

Robert B. Feliciano is a student in the New York City public school system. He has published his poetry in the anthology *Streams 9*.

Isaac Goldemberg was born in Chepén, Peru. In 1964 he moved to New York City, where he now lives. A writer of fiction and poetry, his books include the novels *La vida a plazos de don Jacobo Lerner* and *Tiempo al tiempo*. Among his volumes of poetry are *La vida al contado* and *Hombre de paso/Just Passing Through*. He currently is Distinguished Professor in the Spanish department at Hostos Community College.

David Hernandez has written, recited, and taught poetry for thirty years. He is an active member of Chicago's arts community. He is also the founder of Street Sounds—a performing arts group that infuses poetry and music with folk, jazz, and Afro-Latin elements. Among his books of poetry are *Rooftop Piper*, *Despertando/Waking Up*, and *Satin City Lullaby*. He lives in Chicago.

Yeni Herrera is a very young poet who lives in New York. Says Yeni, "The pages of my notebooks are covered with sketches. If I could just learn to paint nature—flowers, trees, and plants—really well." Her poetry has been published in *The Kids Corner*, a publication of Abraham House in the Bronx, New York.

Oscar Hijuelos holds an M.F.A. in creative writing from the City College of New York and is the author of six novels, including the internationally celebrated *Mr. Ives' Christmas*. His second novel, *The Mambo Kings Play Songs of Love*, won the 1990 Pulitzer Prize in Fiction, earning him the distinction of being the first Latino to win that award. He lives in New York City.

Tato Laviera was born in Santurce, Puerto Rico, and immigrated with his family to New York City at age ten. Before writing poetry he worked as a social services administrator. Among his books of poetry are *La Carreta Made a U-Turn*, *Enclave*, and *AmeRícan*.

Jaime Manrique was born in Colombia. His first book of poems received his country's national book award. He is the author of the novels *Colombian Gold*, *Latin Moon in Manhattan*, and *Twilight at the Equator*. Among his published volumes of poetry are *My Night with Federico García Lorca* and *Tarzan, My Body, Christopher Columbus*. He is an associate professor in the M.F.A. Program at Columbia University.

Willie Perdomo is a poet of the renowned Nuyorican Poets Cafe. He is the author of the poetry volumes *Postcards* of *El Barrio* and *Where a Nickel Costs a Dime,* as well as a picture book, *Visiting Langston.* He has been featured on several PBS documentaries, including *Words in Your Face* and *The United States of Poetry.* He lives in New York.

Amiris Ramirez is a student in the New York City public school system. She has published her poetry in the anthology *Streams 16.*

Luis J. Rodríguez is a poet, journalist, and critic whose works have appeared in *The Nation,* the *Los Angeles Times,* and *Poets and Writers.* He is a Carl Sandburg Literary Award–winner for nonfiction and a Lannan Fellow in poetry. He is also the author of the acclaimed memoir *Always Running: La Vida Loca, Gang Days in L.A.* He resides in California.

Trinidad Sánchez, Jr., is a nationally known Chicano poet and author who lectures extensively at schools, universities, and literary and cultural centers. He is the author of *Why Am I So Brown?* and the chapbooks *Authentic Chicano Food Is Hot* and *Father and Son.* He lives in Colorado.

Raquel Valle Sentíes is a poet, playwright, and painter from Texas. She is the manager of the bookstore El Café del Barrio in Laredo. Her book of poetry *Soy como soy y qué* received the José Fuentes Mares Award in Letras Chicanas in 1997 and was published in the magazine *Weber Studies,* among other publications.

Michele Serros is an award-winning, frequently anthologized poet and commentator. The author of the poetry volume *Chicana Falsa* and the story collection *How to Be a Chicano Role Model,* she has taught poetry in inner-city schools and women's prisons through the PEN Center West's programs. She lives in New York City.

Gary Soto was born and raised in Fresno, California. He is a prolific writer of books of prose, poetry, and drama, including *Buried Onions, Living Up the Street, Baseball in April, Nerdlandia,* and *Local News.* He has written an opera and produced films for Spanish-speaking children. He is the editor of *Pieces of the Heart: New Chicano Fiction.*

Gina Valdés was born in Los Angeles and raised in Mexico and the United States. She has published several books of poetry, including *Comiendo lumbre/Eating Fire* and *Puentes y fronteras/Bridges and Borders.* Her poetry and fiction have appeared in many journals in Mexico, Europe, and the United States. She has taught literature in both English and Spanish at the University of California, San Diego, and San Diego State University. She lives in San Diego's East County.